HE RESTORES
MY SOUL

RECLAIMING WHOLENESS IN YOUR SOUL
DENVA SMITH

HE RESTORES MY SOUL

Unless otherwise indicated, all Scripture quotations are taken from the Holy Bible, New International Version®, NIV®. Copyright © 1973, 1978, 1984, 2011 by Biblica, Inc. ™ Used by permission of Zondervan. All rights reserved worldwide. www.zondervan.com The "NIV" and "New International Version" are trademarks registered in the United States Patent and Trademark Office by Biblica, Inc.™

Printed by CreateSpace, an Amazon.com Company @ www.createspace.com

Copyright © 2018 by Denva Smith

First Edition – First Printing

Book Cover: Tito Jemmott, Jr. - bcgmgp@gmail.com

Graphics: www.canva.com

Interior Design and Editing: Beverly E. Barracks
bebarracks@gmail.com

All Rights Reserved. This book or any portion thereof may not be reproduced or used in any form or any manner whatsoever without the express written permission of the author except for the use of brief quotations in a book review. Please direct all inquiries to: smithdenva21@gmail.com.

ISBN-13: 978-0692085387
ISBN-10: 0692085386

PRINTED IN THE UNITED STATES OF AMERICA

Dedication

I give thanks to the Lord for giving me the opportunity, the motivation and the anointing to write. Lord, may you receive Glory and Praise for every *soul* that will benefit from this ministry.

To every sister or brother by blood or in the Lord who encouraged me to keep writing, Thank You!

Table of Contents

Introduction 1
Chapter 1—Issues of the Soul 3
Chapter 2—Excessive Baggage 15
Chapter 3—The Fragmented Soul 27
Chapter 4—The Wounded Soul 31
Chapter 5—The Sorrowful Soul 39
Chapter 6—The Soul Tied 45
Chapter 7—The Perverted Soul 51
Chapter 8—The Sinful Soul 59
Chapter 9—The Caged Soul 69
Chapter 10—The Fearful Soul 73
Chapter 11—Breaking Generational/Emotional Curses
.... 81
Chapter 12—The Sanctified Soul 89
Chapter 13—The Restored Soul 95
Chapter 14—The Merry/Joyful Soul 99
Chapter 15—The Freed Soul 105
Chapter 16—The Healed Soul 111
Chapter 17—Commanding Wholeness in your Soul 115
Chapter 18—No More Condemnation 121
Chapter 19—Being Transparent: My Story 125

Introduction

Why do some people have hard struggles in life, while others prosper and do well? There could be 101 different reasons why this happens. However, we will look at one of the major reasons and why the difference between these two groups of people can be found in the condition of their *souls*.

Whatever goes on in our souls, will eventually manifest itself in our external conditions and ultimately influence the way we think and progress in life.

Have you ever met that individual who always seems to be going through something; when it's not one thing, it's another? There is always some sort of trial, tribulation, setback, disappointment, lack, sickness or emotional issue that is going on with them. Many times, we blame our issues on everyone and everything else except the real culprit; the *enemy* within.

This is what the word of God says, *"My people are destroyed for lack of knowledge."*— **Hs. 4:6a***(NKJV)*. Knowing where the true issue lies is important, because it is in knowing that we are able to confront, conquer and overcome.

At the end of selected Chapters, I have written a prayer for you to pray. Ask the *Holy Spirit* to identify your issue or issues and allow Him to do His part to bring deliverance, healing, and restoration to your *soul*.

Chapter 1
Issues of the Soul

We have not been the best at paying attention to our souls. Unfortunately, it is sometimes after we have messed up horribly that we come to the realization or admit to the fact that we need help. It doesn't matter how talented, brilliant or anointed we are, if our *souls* are unhealthy, tangled-up or broken, there are bound to be issues that spill over into other areas of our lives.

So often, we see great leaders who fall short in certain areas and as a result bring shame to their families and those who look up to them. Some of us know how to look the part and are even great at playing it too, but we tend to forget the part of us that will ensure an all-around healthy, peaceful and integral package.

The Conflict

The issues that we do not confront, are the ones that give way or legal right to the enemy of our souls. *Robert Henderson*[1] states, *"Any lack of the Kingdom being manifest is because of a legal issue. If we are praying according to the will of God and have prayed for an extended time without results, something legal is standing in the way of the answer. Somewhere in the spirit realm the demonic powers have found a legal right to resist the answer from coming to us."*

Likewise, if you have been trying to succeed all your life and have not, then you need to check what's hindering you. Remember, when we talk about manifesting the Kingdom in this perspective, we are talking about righteousness, joy and the peace of God in every area of our lives. With that being said, we have to be intentional about dealing with the hidden issues in our *souls* and even the ones that are staring us right in the face. It's

---

[1] Author of *"Operating in the Courts of Heaven: Granting God the Legal Right to Fulfill His Passion and Answer Our Prayers."*

time for us to take back all legal rights from the enemy so that we can see God's best manifest in our lives.

What is the Soul?

Since our souls play such a significant role in our prosperity, let's first find out what it is. The *soul* of a man is defined as a *"living being."* This is what the scripture says, *"And the Lord God formed man of the dust of the ground and breathed into his nostrils the breath of life; and man became a living soul"* — **Gn.2:7(KJV)**. God breathed into clay; thus, man came alive with the ability to communicate with Him, love Him, and serve Him.

The word of God says, *"But we have this treasure in jars of clay to show that this all surpassing power is from God and not from us"*— **2Co. 4:7**. This treasure is the breath of God in us and the jar of clay is our body which is the house for our *souls*. Without the breath of God in us, we would be nothing but clay; in other words, we would not be alive without the Breath of God.

God has uniquely designed us as triune beings. We are spirit, we live in a body, and we have a *soul*. The *soul* is so intelligently designed by God, that it can hold a lifetime of memories, good and bad. Unfortunately, it is usually the memories of bad experiences that wound our *souls* and affects us negatively and ultimately alters the quality of our lives. God's original intent was that man would prosper in every area of his life and that is the reason *"God blessed them, and said to them, 'Be fruitful, and increase in number; fill the earth and subdue it. Rule over the fish in the sea and the birds in the sky and over every living creature that moves on the ground.'"*— **Gn. 1:28**.

Unfortunately, the effects of sin impacted Adam and Eve in such a way that it cancelled out what was originally intended by God for them and the entire human race.

Other issues such as demonic spirits can live and sometimes hide in our *souls* to prevent us from experiencing God's goodness and to cause further destruction to us.

Spirits don't have bodies, which makes it illegal for them to operate in the earth, thus they look for a host or a house so that they can operate. This is the reason a person with trauma and brokenness is often easy prey for the demonic spirits.

If you have ever experienced traumas of any kind and have not gone through deliverance and or therapy/counseling, the memory of those traumas is still in your *soul*. These memories affect the *soul* by stealing from us and causing issues in more ways than one.

The *soul* of a man is said to be the middle man between the body and the spirit, our *soul* is what determines whether or not we live a fruitful, and productive life or an unproductive, and hindered life. The fact that God has made us triune beings, means that each part is equally important. One part cannot exist without the other. Therefore, if any of these three parts are not working properly, it creates a disruption in what God intended for our lives.

Our *soul* is the part of us that contains our intellect, our emotions, and our consciousness. Our intellect is the part of the *soul* where understanding takes place. In other words, this is where reasoning happens, where we use our senses, and make decisions; our will.

One part of our *soul* is our affection which has to do with our emotions: love, hate, joy, sadness, happiness, anger etc. This part of our *soul* is the area that the enemy uses against us the most because if he can control our emotions, he can manipulate us to make wrong decisions most of the time. If you begin to take note, you will see that people whose *souls* have been affected negatively often have issues with depression, sadness, unforgiveness, offense, anger and the list goes on.

Another part of our *soul* is our consciousness, this is the part that is controlled by the brain. Our consciousness has to do with our five senses: sight, taste, touch, smell and hearing. This is one of the reasons you can hear a certain music and right away it connects you to a time, place or a person. Sometimes you can smell something that triggers a bad or good memory, and unless they are addressed, the *soul* can hold on to these memories for a lifetime.

When the *soul* is affected by situations such as physical abuse, sexual abuse, domestic violence, abandonment, divorce, hurts, rejections, fear and other life altering trauma, it causes wounds and fragmentations in the *soul*.

Paying attention to this area is important, as the soul is the filter for almost everything we do or become in life. Our health, prosperity, how we think, feel, and make decisions all have to do with the health of our *souls*, therefore, God's intention is for our souls to be made whole and be restored.

JEZEBEL and PYTHON goes after the Emotionally Wounded

Jezebel and Python go after the emotionally wounded. Although the enemy doesn't know all that God has planned for us, he may have an idea that we are called to do great things in the earth. The enemy's plans are to wound us, destroy us and stop us before we can come to the full understanding of who we really are, and as a result, he often sends people into our lives to do just that.

People operating in the spirit of Jezebel often seek for those who are wounded in order to contaminate them and stop that person from walking in their God given purpose.

Persons under this influence will use what looks like kindness to manipulate you, but ultimately will try to destroy your confidence, wear you out, and leave you in a state of dependency upon them. This spirit in operation will slander, accuse, and try to stop you from achieving anything worthwhile. If this spirit catches you when you are down emotionally, it will destroy you and leave you for dead.

Sometimes, some of the issues that one deals with, such as fear, lack, fatigue, dizziness, wanting to run or give up, the inability to function, and struggles in your prayer life, are all the results of this spirit operating against the Believer.

Many times, a person operating in this spirit is great with words and will use words to shut you down, and release fear upon you—if you allow it.

One morning I was awakened from my sleep by a voice that mentioned the word Python. I jumped up and asked, *"what about Python Lord?"* During my time in prayer, the *Holy Spirit* pointed out to me that I was dealing with the Python spirit and that was the cause of certain conflicts I was facing.

During my research, I found out that the ultimate goal of the Python spirit is to stop you from fulfilling your God given purpose in life. The spirit of Python is said to wrap itself around it's victim in order to choke and squeeze out their life. It operates by crushing and destroying the vision, dreams and hopes of its victims. "It robs you of your drive, motivation and overall will to fight, and replaces it with discouragement, hopelessness, and apathy."[2]

The word 'apathy' is defined in the Greek as 'Apalgeo' which means, *"to cease to feel pain for."*[3] Persons whom have been attacked by this spirit will often find themselves fearful, weak and weary. This spirit whispers lies, accusations, and condemnations in your ears so that you can doubt God's word and fall into hopelessness and depression.

One of the ways to recognize if the Python spirit is operating in your life is through your prayer time; are you struggling in prayer? If you are, and are caught without your armor of prayer, faith, and the word of God, it can be devastating for you. I suggest returning to your first love by spending time in God's Presence, His word and in prayer and equally so, you must also separate yourself from anyone operating in this spirit.

---

[2] www.thelordmybanner.com/spirit-of-python

[3] http://biblehub.com/greek/524.htm

Paul and Silas were imprisoned, as a result of the Python spirit, but their deliverance came by way of prayer and praising God **(Read Acts Chapter 16)**, you too must be intentional about prayer and declaring the word of God over your life. The word of God tells us that if you decree a thing, it shall be established unto you.

Also, Jesus says,

"Behold, I have given you the authority to tread on serpents and scorpions, and over all the power of the enemy, and nothing shall hurt you." — **Lk. 10:19(ESV)**.

Jesus told Peter, *"I will give you the keys of the kingdom of heaven; whatever you bind on earth will be bound in heaven, and whatever you loose on earth will be loosed in heaven."* — **Mt. 16:19**.

The writer of Hebrews tells us, *"For the word of God is quick, and powerful, and sharper than any twoedged sword, piercing even to the dividing asunder of soul and spirit, and of the joints and marrow, and is a discerner of the thoughts and intents of the heart."* — **Heb. 4:12(KJV)**.

Since the Python spirit's intent is to also shut you down by stopping your vision, through oppression and weariness, begin to write your vision again. Make declarations and war in prayer over what God has intended for you; He has nothing but good in store for you. Declare what the word of God says, *"He will give you the oil of Joy for the spirit of heaviness."* Fight to get into His Presence, because In God's Presence there is the fullness of Joy, and the Joy of the Lord is what gives you strength.

Chapter 2
Emotional Baggage

My *soul* was troubled with issues on top of issues, and my mind was conditioned to think negatively about almost everything. In those earlier years of my walk with the Lord, I noticed that emphasis was placed more on the spirit-man and how to become a stronger more spiritual Christian. Expressing brokenness or struggles with issues or bad emotions would have more than likely gotten you a strong rebuke or what you would call *"no-nonsense / tough love"* encouragement.

Instead of seeking emotional help, most of my days were spent reading and studying the word, trying to be a better, stronger Christian. Yes, my spirit-man did grow, but for the most part, my *soul* was left unattended. I knew the scriptures, and could quote them, but I kept on having issues that seemed to not go away.

Erroneous teachings among certain groups would often not allow people with major issues in their soul to be accepted. Brokenness was sometimes labeled as immaturity or the person having a bad spirit. Unfortunately, many have been shunned, rejected, talked about, and abused because they were wounded and fragmented. To our detriment, we have learned how to toughen-up to the point where our hearts have become callous; our skin has become so thick, while we waste away from a messy, wounded, bleeding and fragmented *soul*.

Not knowing how to get past what I was going through, I experienced much frustration in my early walk as a Believer. Many times, after leaving church or even ministry events, I would either park someplace and cried because of how broken I felt. Other times, I would go home, lock myself in my room and cry till relief came; usually by way of sleep.

After some time, of doing the same thing, instead of just going home to cry, I found myself talking to the Lord in order to get relief. The time came, when I didn't just cry any longer because I felt hurt or rejected, instead, I realized that I needed to do something about this, and I did; praying and writing became my way of escape.

One day after leaving an event feeling bruised, I sat at my computer desk and began to write. In the midst of writing, the thought came to mind, *"I am not the only one experiencing these issues."* And Suddenly, the light came on! Why not write to help those with the same issues? Thus, I began to write about certain subjects. This was about eight to ten years ago.

The Lord has taken me through sessions and seasons of deliverance, but much of my breakthrough came as I poured out my heart in prayer, in fasting, as I studied God's Word and in writing down my thoughts. In the scheme of things, there were issues of my heart that I had to come to terms with, mindsets that had to be released, as well as people that I had to forgive, both deceased and alive. During this season, the *Holy Spirit* also taught me that praying for others was a huge part of my healing and deliverance— *"Then, when Job prayed for his friends, the Lord restored his wealth and happiness!"* —**Job 42:10a *(TLB)*;** and finally, I had to do some repentance on my part.

At this point in my life my personal mandate from the Lord and scripture reference for my ministry is,

"The Spirit of the Lord God is upon me; because the Lord hath anointed me to preach good tidings unto the meek; he hath sent me to bind up the brokenhearted, to proclaim liberty to the captives, and the opening of the prison to them that are bound; To proclaim the acceptable year of the Lord, and the day of vengeance of our God; to comfort all that mourn;" — **Is. 61:1,2 *(KJV)*.**

We are typically not the best at paying attention to ourselves. Unfortunately, it is sometimes after we have messed up horribly that we come to the realization or admit to the fact that we need help.

It doesn't matter how talented, brilliant or anointed we are, if our souls are unhealthy, bound up, or broken, there are bound to be issues that spill over into other areas of our lives.

As Believers of Jesus Christ, God wants us whole in our *souls*. Salvation came to do exactly that; Salvation is paramount to who we are as Believers. There are several words in Hebrew that defines Salvation. One such word is *"Yesha"*[4] - it means deliverance, rescue, salvation, safety, welfare, liberty, victory, health, among other definitions. Another word for Salvation is the word *"Yeshua"* which is another name for Jesus. We know that there is no Salvation without Yeshua/Jesus Christ, for the word of God tells us that there is no other Name under Heaven given among men, whereby we must be Saved **(Ac. 4:12)**.

---

[4] http://biblehub.com/hebrew/strongs_3468.htm

SHALOM SHALOM!

When Jesus came, He did not only come to save us from our sins, but He also came to restore us to a state of Shalom. This word is so packed that when we say *"Shalom"* to someone, we are literally pronouncing upon them all that they could ever need in this life. This word *"Shalom"* has more than one meaning, all of which are necessary to have wholeness in our such as peace, harmony, wholeness, completeness, prosperity, happiness, good health, favor, safety, rest, perfection, welfare and tranquility — **(NAS Exhaustive Concordance)**. These are also some of the same words that define *Yesha*, *Yeshuah*, and *Salvation*.

If you should ask, many Believers would tell you that they are not experiencing the *"Shalom"* mentioned in the word of God, instead they are experiencing lack, not just on a financial level, but also on an emotional, physical, and spiritual level. Many are frustrated, because they are not aware why they are struggling, but more often, the main factor is the issue of the wounded *soul*. Jesus by way of the Cross, already made provision for all our wounds, both physical and emotional — **(See Is. 53:5)**.

The word of God tells us "For in Christ all the fullness of the Deity dwells in bodily form. And we have been made complete (whole, perfect, victorious) in Christ." — **Col 2:9,10**. Since we have been made complete in Him, we need to be experiencing this wholeness.

The Core of the Issue

I have a friend who had a wound on her foot for some time. She saw many doctors and after a period of time, they got her foot to the place where it started to heal. About a year or so down the road, she started having problems with the same wound all over again. Her doctors eventually figured out the root of the issue and were able to treat her foot so that it would heal.

However, my friend ended up in rehab in order for her foot to heal properly. One day I went to visit her at the rehab facility, and out of nowhere she started explaining what happened to her foot, and the process it would have to undergo in order to heal properly. She said,

"Pat, let me explain to you what's going on here. The doctors said that I had what you call a false healing or pseudo-healing. Although my foot looked like nothing was wrong with it, it was festering on the inside, while the outer skin looked normal and other parts were getting callus. In order for my foot to heal, the doctors had to scrape and drain the infected flesh as well as the bone."

How **PAINFUL** I thought; in other words, *"the infection went deep down to the bone."*

When she began telling me this, all I thought about was the state of the wounded *soul*, and how this situation described the issue to it's very core. We look like we are whole, but underneath the mask and facade, we have terrible, life altering wounds.

No More Cover Up

Many of us are wounded to the core of our beings and need divine intervention from God. We can no longer cover up or pretend that we are okay, because it comes out in all kinds of ways. The word of God tells us that out of the abundance of the heart *(soul)* the mouth speaks.

Do you gossip all the time, are you oftentimes sad, timid, angry, jealous, fearful, prideful, always finding fault with others or do you put up walls to keep others out? If you answered yes to any of these, then there's a great possibility, that there are issues in your *soul*. Issues such as molestation, rape, physical abuse, abandonment, accidents, rejection, traumas of any kind, or even surgeries. If yes, then you may be experiencing woundedness in your *soul*. Freedom comes only when we are able to admit that something is wrong and seek help. We are free when we no longer have to wear masks, but instead be our true authentic self!

So many have not seen answers to their prayers and are mad at God. They believe that

He is withholding the 'good' from them. The Bible says, *"No good thing will I withhold from them who walk uprightly."* — **Ps.84-11**. While others believe that God prefers other people over them and that's the reason for them not having answers to their prayers. Be assured that the word of God is Truth — *"Then Peter began to speak: 'I now realize how true it is that God does not show favoritism but accepts from every nation the one who fears him and does what is right.'"*— **Ac. 10:34,35**. God is, however, moved by our Faith.

Our finances/prosperity is one of the major areas that suffers as a result of issues in the soul- The Bible tells us that we prosper as our *soul* prospers. Although finances are not the only thing that defines prosperity, it is a big part of it.

Our health can be affected just as well, because the Bible says a wounded *soul* dries up the bone. Not only that, but a lot of our ailments can be traced back to our woundedness or the trauma that we may have experienced.

If you find yourself being angry with God, don't be! Why? Because God loves us all with an everlasting love. We cannot perform enough or be good enough to earn God's love or favor. He promised to do us good, and His promises are based on His unconditional love for us. The word of God tells us that all His promises are Yes, and in Him, Amen. — **2Co. 1:20**. This means that whatever promises God has made in His word, once we are in Christ, they belong to us too.

When we make the decision to deal with the issues in our *souls*, we will begin to see breakthroughs in every area of our lives. The word of God says, *"Beloved, I pray that all may go well with you and that you may be in good health, as it goes well with your soul."*— **3Jn. 1:2***(ESV)*.

The word of God is the most vital remedy for the healing of the *soul*. **Jms. 1:21**— tells us that we are to get rid of the filth and evil in our lives and humbly accept the word of God which is able to save-(SOZO) our *souls*.

God knows exactly what it will take to bring our healing. He is ready to release His *supernatural* healing power to heal our fragmented *souls* and bring us back to a state of Shalom (Completeness, Soundness, Welfare, and Success).

One of the promises that God has given us in His word is that He, the good Shepherd will restore our *souls*. It is, therefore, important that we first and foremost know that the Lord is our Shepherd, because His promises are for those who are in covenant with Him. — **Psa. 23:1-3a** says, *"The Lord is my Shepherd, I shall not want. He maketh me to lie down in green pastures: He leadeth me besides the still waters. He restoreth my soul;"*

The good Shepherd is and has always been ready to restore our *souls*. The enemy doesn't want you and I to know what's affecting our *souls*, so that he can keep us in a state of brokenness, but we must ask the Spirit of God to reveal those hidden areas so that they can be addressed.

Chapter 3
The Fragmented Soul

Each traumatic situation that we go through in life, causes breakage in our *souls*. When someone goes through a separation, whether from a spouse, a mother, a father, a friend or it could be the loss of something that is dear to us, it is said to break the heart. The 'heart' that I am speaking of is not the physical one that pumps in our chest, in fact, it is the Hebrew word— *lebab/leb*[5] which is another name for the *soul*; it is the seat of our emotion or the inner man.

When something is fragmented, it's not just broken, it's shattered. The word fragmentation[6] is defined as— *"a state of breaking or being broken into small or separate parts."* In other words, the

---

[5] www.preceptaustin.org/heart_leb

[6] https://www.thefreedictionary.com/fragmentation

thing that is fragmented will be harder to be put back together and will take more time.

Some of the causes of fragmentation in the *soul* are: traumas, music—yes music, drugs, adultery, fornication or any sexual sins, negative generational patterns, occult practices, soul ties, among other things.

To begin the healing process, we must first commit our emotions, will, and intellect to God. We must renounce, repent and turn away from things, such as ungodly music, sexual sins, *soul* ties and generational curses. For some of us, the word of God is all that will be needed, because it washes, heals, and saves the *soul*. For others we must go through deliverance, from traumas, occult practices, drugs and alcohol, etc.

One of the things that we must understand, however, is that God is ever so near to the brokenhearted, and He saves those who are crushed in spirit.

Your heart may be broken and your spirit may be crushed, but it cannot be so destroyed that God cannot restore you. No matter how fragmented you are, God is able to put you back together again.

PRAYER:

Father, in Jesus Name, I present my fragmented soul to You. I ask Your forgiveness for all my sins. I renounce soul ties and evil generational spirits and practices that caused fragmentation of my soul. I repent and turn away from every sin and ungodly lifestyle. I will wait for You Father God, because Salvation comes from You. Bring together all the fragmented parts of my soul that were taken from me and restore the parts that were given away out of ignorance and heal me in Jesus Name I Pray. Amen!

Chapter 4
The Wounded Soul

The *soul* can be wounded from many different sources. Just to name a few, there are Father wounds, Mother wounds, wounds that have been inflicted by family members, wounds from friends, wounds from sin, wounds from our enemies and so much more.

When the *soul* is wounded, it is not prospering, therefore, it affects our emotional state, our health, our mental state, our money, our ability to move forward, among other things. *We hear, see, and perceive everything through a broken filter.*

A wounded *soul* often misses God, because of the lack of trust, fear, pride, unforgiveness, doublemindedness and the inability to receive from Him. Why? Sometimes, we can't see God as the kind, loving, caring, merciful, protective, giving Father that He really is, because we think if He were all those things, why am I not better? So instead, we see ourselves as orphans.

A wounded *soul* is one of the hardest issues to deal with. That person feels pain in their emotions that spills over into other areas of their lives. The sad reality is that one cannot take a pill to stop that pain, although many have tried. You can't go to the hospital and tell them you are hurting in your *soul*. If you do, you will more than likely be admitted to the **psych ward**.

When someone has a physical wound, it prohibits physical functionality on a daily basis. Sometimes that physical wound, if not attended to carefully, can be infected causing the person further pain and problems. Likewise, with emotional wounds, if not attended to, it can hinder emotional functionality and can put a halt to your life, preventing you from experiencing healthy progression.

A wound is defined as, *"an injury to living tissue caused by a cut, blow or other impact, typically one in which the skin is cut or broken."*[7] Words that are synonymous with wound are: injury, lesion, cut, gash, laceration, tear, slash, graze, scratch, abrasion, contusion, and trauma. We can also use these words to describe the different kinds of wounds. Sometimes that wound may have come in the form of childhood molestation, physical abuse, or domestic violence.

People can be wounded in so many different ways. For instance, when it's a cut, most times it comes by way of words. Words from parents released out of ignorance, negative words from friends, and family members; God help us, if they came from a spiritual leader.

The words that come from natural or spiritual leaders alike seem to cut deeper and harder. Those words can sometimes be so damaging that it leaves the recipient wounded, bleeding, and without hope. These kinds of

---

[7] https://www.google.com/wound

wounds make one angry and bitter and it sometimes causes doors to be opened to other toxic emotions. If those words are not uprooted, and rendered null and void, they can literally cause one's life to be shipwrecked.

On the other hand, leaders can release words that are constructive and intended to bring correction, but if those words are not released and seasoned with grace and love, they can also wound. The Bible talks about Jesus, and how He was full of Truth and Grace; in other words, Truth was not given in a way that would cause more harm instead; Grace was given along with Truth.

Sometimes we have to take even the harsh words and make the necessary adjustments. We must know the difference between the two intentions, and when they are constructive, we must receive even the harsh word with meekness, because God is using them to make us better.

For example, a tear, slash, gash, bruise, laceration, contusion, lesion or trauma could also describe different ways in which the *soul* gets wounded.

- A tear could be described from the loss of a loved one, a divorce, or the breakup of a love relationship.

- A slash could be the loss of a friendship or the loss of an object.

- A gash could be a deadly word or plot released against you.

- A bruise could be something that you would rather not hear, "he said, she said" or even an offense; "a bruised ego."

- A laceration could be good or bad; the word of God says, faithful are the wounds of a friend or *"wounds from a sincere friend are better than many kisses from an enemy."* — **Pr. 27:6 (NLT)**.

- A contusion could be a situation that hits you unexpectedly, sometimes not to destroy you, but to put a halt to your progress.

- A lesion could be something that has attached itself to your emotions, such as rejection, pride, anger, fear, unforgiveness, etc.

- Trauma could come in all kind of ways, molestation, rape, accidents of any forms, abandonment, physical abuse and so much more.

The word of God says, *"The spirit of a man will sustain him in sickness, but who can bear a broken spirit (soul)?"* — **Pr. 18:14***(NKJV)*.

Two of the remedies that are often used for people with wounds are counseling or therapy. I say yes to both of them, but there are parts of our *souls* that are so entrenched in bad memories of bad experiences that it will take the *supernatural* work of the *Holy Spirit* to bring deliverance, healing and wholeness.

The word of God is paramount for the healing of our wounded *souls*, **(Jms. 1:21)** tells us that the word of God has to be poured in like water, and it washes. Other times the word of God has to be taken like a regimen or medication; in other words, confess it to your *souls*; it has the Power to Save.

Sometimes, it takes laying hands on and speaking over you to uproot, cast out, and erase certain memories. In the meantime, allow the Spirit of God to start the work in you with this prayer.

PRAYER:

Father, in the Name of Jesus, I lift up my soul to You. I ask You to deliver me from brokenness. Heal me of every wound that was inflicted upon me by the enemy of my soul. Remove from my soul the memory of past pains and griefs that have left me wounded. I ask You to break the power of the Words that were released against me and have hindered me or have framed my mindset in a negative way. Deliver me from toxic emotions that have infected my soul. Help me to renew my mind so that I can receive my breakthrough in the area of my soul. Father, I am asking You to deliver me from the mentality that has kept me wounded, bound and stagnant in my life. I give You thanks in advance for my breakthrough, in Jesus Name. Amen!

Chapter 5
The Sorrowful Soul

A sorrowful *soul* can also be termed as *"broken heart syndrome"* as is defined by the Mayo Clinic. It is said to be *"a temporary heart condition that's often brought on by stressful situations, such as the death of a loved one. The condition can also be triggered by a serious physical illness or surgery. People with broken heart syndrome may have sudden chest pain or think they're having a heart attack."*[8]

Sorrow can come as a result of painful situations. Sorrow also comes in different degrees; some people may be sorrowful because they lost loved ones, some mourn because they lost relationships, and others mourn because of sin, while there are those who mourn because they were caught. The

---

[8] https://www.mayoclinic.org/diseases-conditions/broken-heart-syndrome/symptoms-causes

sorrow that one feels because of sin is good, as it should lead one to repentance. The word of God says that godly sorrow leads to repentance.

People mourn when they have lost loved ones. For example, when my husband died, I couldn't come to terms with it. Although I didn't mourn outwardly, unbeknownst to me, my *soul* was affected badly and sorrow was sitting in my *soul* waiting to manifest itself in different ways. Five years down the road, my mother went home to be with the Lord, and again I tried to get away from mourning outwardly. Not long after, I found myself having recurring panic attacks. My chest would become tight, which made breathing very uneasy. Night-after-night, I would end up in the emergency room thinking that I was going to die.

On occasions, I would breakdown and weep, because I missed my loved ones, but would quickly clean-up, so no one would know that I was suffering inwardly.

One night while I was being ministered to, the spirit of grief was located and commanded to leave my *soul*. After that, the panic attacks stopped, but sorrow lingered to a certain degree. Then, one Sunday morning in our local church, my Apostles called out that sorrowful spirit and commanded it to be broken for good; to God be the Glory!

The sorrow that comes as a result of a broken friendship can be as devastating as that which comes with the loss of a loved one. It is always important for people to grieve properly so that it will not affect the *soul* negatively.

Sorrow is a healthy part of grieving a loss, but it can become unhealthy when we fail to allow the natural process to take place. Not grieving none at all, is just as bad as grieving for too long; they both affect the *soul* negatively. The word of God tells us, *"Blessed are those who mourn, for they shall be comforted."* — **Mt. 5:4***(NKJV)*.

For every person who may be experiencing sorrow or grief, I command that sorrow to leave your *soul* right now in Jesus Name! I declare and decree that even as you are reading this book, healing is taking place in your *soul*, in Jesus Name. I encourage you to speak to your *soul* and make declarations concerning your having a healthy *soul*.

David spoke to his *soul*; these are his words, why are you so sorrowful within me oh my *soul*? hope in God! — **Ps. 43:5**. Likewise, I am encouraging you to speak to your *soul*. Don't lose your faith and hope in God. God is with you in whatever you are sorrowful about.

Use the word of God to strengthen your *soul*, as the word mends, it heals and it *will* restore your joy. Don't just use mere words but use the word of God.

Praising God is another way to get your healing from sorrow. These are David's words of Praise to God. *"You have turned for me my mourning into dancing; you have put off my sackcloth (mourning clothes) and clothed me with gladness, To the end that my glory may sing praise to you and not be silent. O Lord my God, I will give thanks to you forever."* — **Ps. 30: 11,12**(*NKJV*).

Another way to get your freedom from a sorrowful *soul* is to be Thankful. We are not trying to be thankful for the death of a loved one or for the end of a relationship, but we are to be thankful in spite of. The word of God tells us that in everything, we are to be thankful; for this is the Will of God in Christ Jesus for you. —**1Th. 5:18**(*NKJV*). Let's pray,

PRAYER:

Father, in Jesus Name, I thank You for my life. I thank you that You are with me. You never leave me or forsake me. Today, I surrender my pain, grief and sorrows to You. I am asking You to heal me from the effects of every loss that I have experienced. Fill those empty spaces with Your grace and love. I decree over my life that sorrow is fleeing from me now in Jesus Name. No longer will my soul be cast down. Today I hope in You; today I joy in You; my strength is in You. In You I live, move and have my very being. Turn for me Father my mourning into dancing. I put off my mourning clothes and I'm asking You to clothe me with gladness. I will sing Praises to You most high God and will tell of Your goodness. In Jesus Name I Pray. Amen!

Chapter 6
The Soul Tied

Often when we hear the words, *"soul tie,"* we think negatively about it. However, *soul ties* are not always a negative thing. There are healthy *soul ties* and there are unhealthy *soul ties*. A wife's *soul* should be tied to her husbands. Gn. 2: 24 — talks about a man leaving his mother and father and becoming one with his wife. How does this happen? It takes place in the *soul*; their *souls* have become intertwined with one another, therefore, becoming one.

Another example of heathy *soul ties* in the Bible is that of Naomi and Ruth. We know from scriptures that Naomi, her husband and two sons went to a place called Moab during a time of famine. Her husband died and she was left with her two sons who went on to marry two Moabite women. Time went by and both sons died and left the women widowed. The famine was over in Judah and thus Naomi headed back home. One of the daughter's-in-law stayed in Moab, while the other vowed to go with her mother-in-law. The word says, Ruth clung to Naomi, and here are her famous words,

"Don't urge me to leave you or to turn back from you. Where you go I will go, and where you stay I will stay. Your people will be My people and your God my God. Where you die I will die, and there I will be buried. May the Lord deal with me, ever so severely, if even death separates you and me." — **Ru. 1-16,17b**.

Ruth went on later to marry Boaz, a family member of Naomi's husband and had children.

The moral of this story is that there are people that God will allow your *souls* to be divinely connected with because great purpose will come from it. Ruth in her spirit knew that there was great purpose in being connected to Naomi, thus she stayed close to her. As we now know, Jesus, the Savior of the world, came out of the bloodline of Boaz and Ruth. Thus, we see the powerful result of heathy *soul ties*.

Soul ties can also be bad, unhealthy, and dangerous. If your *soul* is *tied* up with the wrong person, it can totally derail your future and purpose. Both men and women alike must be careful about the relationships that they enter into, because with each person you connect with, you give them part of your *soul* and likewise, you take part of theirs.

The enemy can bring people in our lives that are disguised as friends but are really on assignment from hell to stop you from moving forward or to hijack your purpose in life. I even heard my Apostles talking about having *soul ties* to a ministry or establishment. If it's the ministry or establishment that God wants you in, then by all means, lend your supply, not only that, but you will be able to receive from that ministry what God has intended for you to receive. But if it's not the ministry that you should be connected to or your season is up, then being tied there can be detrimental to your moving forward in God.

We can fearlessly welcome healthy *soul ties*, which are relationships that God has divinely connected us to, but we must renounce all unhealthy *soul ties*, and whatever covenant that was made out of ignorance, and ask God to loose us from them.

PRAYERS:

Father, In the Name of Jesus, son of the living God, I thank You for every healthy and productive relationship that You have connected me with. I thank You in advance for the purpose for which You have connected me to these relationships. I ask You for the wisdom that I will need to remain in these divine connections, help me to develop honor for these connections and cut off every cord that connects me to the wrong relationships. I break and sever every unhealthy soul tie. I renounce all unhealthy emotions or emotional connections to anyone that I am not married to, or divinely connected to. Bring back the parts of my soul that I have given out of ignorance and restore the parts that were taken illegally. I declare freedom in my soul and I say that nothing or no one can hold me bound.

Father, I ask You to divinely connect me with those whom You have purposed to be in my life. Cause me to be a blessing to them and cause them to be a blessing to me. I declare that there will be no competition amongst us, because we are connected to build the same Kingdom. Bless all my divine connections and cause divine explosions and divine inspirations when we collaborate concerning your Kingdom, in Jesus Name. Amen!

Chapter 7
The Perverted Soul

It really doesn't take a whole lot for a person's *soul* to become perverted. All it takes is perverted music, perverted movies, perverted conversations or acts of perversion to cause corruption in the *soul*.

What is perversion?

Webster's Dictionary defines perversion as *"a diverting from the true intent or purpose; a change to something worse; a turning or applying to a wrong end or use."*[9]

When a *soul* has become perverted, there is literally no restraint on what this person will do. Adultery, fornication, masturbation, unholy fantasies, homosexuality, pornography, rape, molestation, and corrupt communication

---

[9] https://www.gotquestions.org/Bible-perversion.html

to name a few, are all forms of the spirit of perversion.

Perversion takes place when we allow our eyes and our ears to be open to what is perverse. Perversion can enter our *souls* when we are connected to a perverted person. It can also come in when someone has been violated, be it in childhood or adulthood.

Proverbs 6:32,33 tells us, *"But a man who commits adultery has no sense; whoever does so destroys himself. Blows and disgrace are his lot, and his shame will never be wiped away."*

Perversion causes destruction in many ways, bringing with it disgrace and shame. Perversion doesn't only affect the person being influenced by it, but also the people connected to the perverted person. No wonder the Bible tell us to flee or run from it because it opens the door to a curse

The word of God says this, *"One whose heart is corrupt does not prosper; one whose tongue is perverse falls into trouble."* — **Pr. 17:20**.

As Believers, we must take heed to the word of God, *"But among you there must not be even a hint of sexual immorality, or any kind of impurity, or of greed, because these are improper for God's holy people. Nor should there be obscenity, foolish talk or coarse joking, which are out of place, but rather thanksgiving. For of this you can be sure: no immoral, impure or greedy person-such a person is an idolater-has any inheritance in the kingdom of Christ and of God."*— **Eph. 5:3-5**.

1. How do we get freedom and stay free from a perverted *soul*?

    a. Ask God for deliverance.

    b. Stay away from the source of perversion.

    c. Spend time in the word of God.

    d. Spend time in fasting.

    e. Pray and spend much time in the Presence of God.

    f. Get accountability partners or someone who you can be accountable to.

    g. Ask others to pray for you.

Right now, you may be apprehensive about sharing your struggles with other Believers, fearing that you will be ostracized. Suffice to say that God has people in the body who can be trusted with these situations; these are people who will sincerely pray, love, and cover you no matter what. The word of God tells us that love covers a multitude of sins, so know that there are those whom God has assigned to cover you.

2. How do we protect our *souls* from perversion?

   The word of God says *"Keep your heart (soul) with all diligence, for out of it spring the issues of life."* — **Pr.4:23(NKJV)**.

   Our eyes, ears and mouths are gates to and from our *souls*, therefore:

   a. We protect our eye gates by being careful of what we allow ourselves to see or watch.

      In the same way that I try to protect my children's imagination when certain filth comes on the television, it is the same way I protect mine. If a movie is rated R, I won't be seeing it until it has been modified.

In fact, whatever we look at continuously, that's the thing we draw to ourselves or we draw closer to. We must remember that we host the Spirit of God, which means He is always with us. Whatever we see, He sees. Whatever we hear, He hears. Whatever we do, we join the Spirit of God to that thing.

b. We protect our ear gates by being careful what we allow ourselves to hear or deliberately listen to.

If you are a single, saved individual and still listen to certain secular music, how do you expect to be delivered from a life of fornication; or wanting to have intimate relations?

Our *souls* are like computers, whatever we allow in, stays in. Even when we erase certain things, the experts could always go deeper and find what we have erased on the hard drive. Likewise, everything that we allow in, stays in, unless God *supernaturally* removes it.

c. We protect our mouth gate, by being careful of what we say. When we talk foolishly or engage in coarse jesting like the word of God mentioned, we are perverting our *souls*. Gossip, and slander also perverts our *souls*, therefore, be careful what you are allowing to come out of your mouth.

Sometimes, it is the things that still linger in our *souls* that cause us to curse, slander or gossip. The word of God tells us that out of the abundance of our hearts (*souls*) the mouth speaks. — **Lk. 6:45**.

When we gossip, curse or engage in unholy speech, we are literally bringing out what had been stored up in our *souls*. We can use our mouths to pervert our *souls* or we can use it to bring deliverance to our *souls* and to others.

PRAYER:

Father, in the Name of Jesus, I come to You surrendering my soul and all that lies within me. I ask You to remove everything that would pervert my soul and lead me deeper into sin. Help me to guard my heart with all diligence like You admonished in your word and help me to speak that which would be beneficial to me and to others. Bring Your light to every dark and hidden area of my soul and help me to be careful about what comes from my mouth in Jesus Name. Amen!

Chapter 8
The Sinful Soul

Mankind on a whole is sinful! As a result of the fall, we were all born with the natural inclination to sin. Sin is one of those things that wound our *souls*; as a result, we all need deliverance from sin wounds. According to the word of God, we were all born in sin and shaped in iniquity. Jesus Christ took on our infirmities, weaknesses and wounds on the Cross, and as a result, we were healed. — **Is. 53:5**.

As soon as you and I say yes to Jesus Christ and the finished work of the Cross, we immediately receive our healing from sin. We are then translated from death unto life, but our *souls* will need deliverance from the wounds that sin inflicted.

After the transition from death to life in Christ, we should no longer have the sin nature, because when we allow Christ to come in, He makes all things new according to the word of God. *"Therefore, if anyone is in Christ, he is a new creation. The old has passed away; behold, the new has come."* — **2 Cor. 5:17*(ESV)*.** Now that we have the mind of Christ, we can now begin to set our affections on things above where Christ is seated at the right hand of the Father; we have now become the righteousness of God in Christ.

Many have found themselves in sin patterns that are generational. They did not open up to it, nor did they sign up for it, they just found themselves struggling in certain areas without explanation.

There was a time in the past when we would have to pay for the sins of our forefathers, and even now, people have found themselves struggling with generational sins and wondering why the struggle.

"The Lord is slow to anger, abounding in love and forgiving sin and rebellion. Yet he does not leave the guilty unpunished; he punishes the children for the sin of the parent to the third and fourth generation." — **Nm. 14:18**.

The word of the Lord came to Jeremiah saying, *"In those days people will no longer say, 'The parents have eaten sour grapes, and the children's teeth are set on edge.' Instead, everyone will die for their own sin; whoever eats sour grapes- their own teeth will be set on edge."* — **Jr. 31:29,30**.

Now we know, that the reason we don't have to pay for the sins of our forefathers is because Jesus came and **Paid the Price**.

When a *soul* is in a state of continuously sinning, that person is considered dead to the life in Christ and alive to sin. Sin blocks and separates us from God, and only the blood of Jesus Christ can bring reconciliation. *"Sin has a diminishing factor to it. It always gives its best in the beginning. It never gets better after that it only gets worst,"* — **Mark Aulson**.

People find themselves in different states of sin, and there are different kinds of sin. The Bible even talks about a sin that leads to death and one that does not.

1. The *soul* in sin who has never come into the knowledge of Christ.

   The Gospel of Jesus Christ must be shared with those who are lost, for it is the Power of God unto Salvation — **Rm. 1:16**. Also, he that wins *souls* is wise — **Pr. 11:30**. It is God's Will that all men be Saved!

2. Those who are Believers, but have struggled with an area of sin in their *soul*.

   With these people, the word of God says, we are to restore them in love. *"Brothers and sisters, if someone is caught in a sin, you who live by the Spirit should restore that person gently. But watch yourselves, or you may also be tempted. Carry each other's burdens, and in this way you will fulfill the law of Christ."* — **Gl. 6:1,2**.

God does not want us to be critical, harsh or judgmental to those who are struggling with sin, but have a desire to be delivered. Too often, people find themselves in unwanted struggles, as a result of sin and iniquities that came down through their generation. Whatever the case may be, we who are spiritual need to be in a restorative mode to restore God's people.

3. For the person who confesses Christ and continues to live in blatant sin without any regard for God or man, this is the *soul* that the word of God says shall surely die. — **Ezk. 18:4**. If you have confessed Jesus Christ as your Savior, and nothing about you has changed, again, you must check yourself to see if you are really of the faith.

There are no boundaries for the *soul* that lives in sin. *"It will take you further than you want to go, keeps you longer than you want to stay and cost more than you want to pay."* — **Mark Aulson**.

Sin will destroy your *soul*, cut your life short, and sometimes unfortunately, claim the lives of your loved ones; this is the word of God to people who are in this state,

"If we deliberately keep on sinning after we have received the knowledge of the truth, no sacrifice for sin is left, but only a fearful expectation of judgement and of raging fire that will consume the enemies of God."— **Heb. 10:26,27**.

There is a big difference between the person who is struggling with sin, and one who lives in a state of sin. If you are a Believer, and you have been living a life of sin, then first, you need to examine yourself to see if you are really of the faith according to Paul.

"Examine yourselves to see whether you are in the faith; test yourselves. Do you not realized that Christ Jesus is in you- unless, of course, you fail the test?" — **2 Co.13:5**.

Paul also cautioned us not to continue in sin just because we know that God's grace is available. We are to make no provision for the flesh, because the more that we feed the flesh is the more the flesh will need.

"What shall we say then? Shall we go on sinning so that grace may increase?" And his answer is, *"God forbid!"* We must understand that when we say that we are Children of God and we continue to do what is displeasing to Him, we are literally hurting His heart. It time for a true turnaround.

PRAYERS:

If you have never accepted Jesus Christ as your Savior, please pray this prayer.

God in Heaven, I come to You as best I know how. I am a sinner and need Your Salvation. I believe that You sent Your Son to die on the Cross for my sins. I believe that He died and rose from the dead and is now alive with You in Heaven. Jesus, I ask You to come into my heart, forgive me of all my sins, wash me in Your Blood. And now, I confess that I am Saved. Read **Rm. 10:9,10**.

If you are a person that has been struggling with sin and want change, please pray this prayer:

Father God, In the Name of Jesus Christ, I come to You. I present my body as a living sacrifice to You, and I surrender my soul to You. Please forgive me for hurting Your Heart by my actions. I am asking You to deliver me from all carnal weaknesses and sin. Please remove everyone and everything that is detrimental to my walk with You. Grant me the power to say no to sin and to turn to You in times of weakness. I surrender all that I am to You, and I say that I belong to You. Thank You for my freedom from a life of sin. In Jesus Name. Amen!

This prayer is for the one who has confessed Christ as Savior and Lord and has continued to live a life of sin. If you are willing to change, this prayer is for you. The word of God tells us that if we are willing and obedient, we will eat the good of the land. Know that God does not expect you to fix things on your own, all He is looking for is the one who will say Yes to Life. He will do the part that you can't do. God is able to keep you if you want to be kept.

The word of God says this, *"Now unto him that is able to keep you from falling, and to present you faultless before the presence of his glory with exceeding joy, To the only wise God our Savior, be glory and majesty, dominion and power, both now and forever. Amen."*— **Jd. 1:24,25(KJV)**.

PRAYER:

Father God, in the Name of Your Son Jesus Christ, I come to You. I have been living a life that is contrary to Your will and I'm asking You to forgive me. I repent of all ungodly lifestyles, and I surrender myself totally and completely to You. I ask Your forgiveness for anyone who I may have turned away from You by the life I lived.

Your word promises me that You are able to keep me from falling, so please keep me from falling. I renounce generational sins and iniquities that have come down through my bloodline. I am asking You to clothe me in righteousness and make all things new. In Jesus Name, I Pray. Amen!

Chapter 9
The Caged Soul

There are some people who have gone through such traumatic circumstances that the enemy has held them hostage emotionally. Some have been held as a result of generational curses. *Souls* that are caged in by deep depression; *souls* that are caged in by bitterness, resentment, and unforgiveness. *Souls* that are caged in by witchcraft, hexes, and vexes, *souls* caged by schizophrenia and bipolar disorder; and sometimes the *soul* is caged by wrong mindsets and vain imaginations.

These are *souls* that God cares about. God said in His word, *"All souls are mine."* So many are locked up not just in emotional cages, but they are also locked away in physical cages called asylums and mental institutions.

One of the things that we have to do as Believers, is to pray for those who the enemy has caged in these ways. Believe it or not, many of those whom the enemy has caged in this way are those with the Calling of God on their lives; those who the enemy knows will cause a blow to His Kingdom.

God wants us as Believers to pray for these *souls*. Sometimes they are our loved ones or family members, and for some, they are just people that we may or may not know personally. One way or the other, we have the power to command them to be loosed from every cage that holds them hostage.

We can command these chains to be broken and that they be set Free in Jesus Name!

"The Spirit of the Sovereign Lord is on me, because the Lord has anointed me to proclaim good news to the poor. He has sent me to bind up the brokenhearted, to proclaim freedom for the captives and release from darkness for the prisoners…" — *Read* **Is. 61:1**.

Sometime it's the words of leaders and other people that put us in bondage. There are folks in secret who do evil chants and speak wicked words against others, even the people of God. God Himself says in His word that He would deliver His people out of the hands of those who practice divination, and they, the diviners, shall know that He is God. — **Ezk. 13:23**.

Let's pray for those who are bound in cages, in mental and emotional prisons. If you are the one who needs this prayer, then go ahead and pray it for yourself.

PRAYER:

Father, in the Name of Jesus, we come to You on behalf of those who are caged, bound, or imprisoned mentally and emotionally. We send Your word to lose them now from every chain that has them bound. We bind spirits that traffic their minds, in Jesus Name. Deliver them from every cage and prison that has entrapped and bound them. We declare clarity of mind, healing of their broken hearts, and freedom in every area of their souls. Break the powers of hell from off of them, break every word of witchcraft, and set them free by the blood of Jesus Christ. Restore everything that was stolen from them. Restore their souls, restore their families, restore their monies, restore their health, restore the years that were stolen from them and much more. We declare Your shalom over them and we say that they are Free in Jesus Name. Amen!

Chapter 10
The Fearful Soul

As a child I was crippled by the spirit of fear. In fact, most of my life was spent in fear. This spirit plagued me and prevented me from doing anything that would bring advancement in my life. Looking back, I wondered and even asked the Lord to show me at what point this fear entered my life. The Spirit of God began to pinpoint to me some of my most vulnerable moments where the enemy gained access and came in.

Fear enters the *soul* in so many different ways. When it enters, it holds the *soul* hostage. This fear can be so crippling that it cheats one out of living a normal and free life.

One of the agendas of fear is to stop us from walking in the freedom and the authority that Christ has given us through the Cross. It is to stop us from walking in greatness. It stops us from receiving and experiencing the Love of God.

I remembered as a child, living with my grandparents, we had certain chores that we had to get done before they got home. My grandparents usually got home at about 11 o'clock at night. If they came home and our chores weren't done, we would have to get up and do them no matter how late it was or how tired we were.

Now, we did not live in an area that was well lit nor did we have neighbors nearby. We lived in a beautiful area surrounded by thick bushes, deep valleys and sugar cane fields. We had dogs and at night, we would hear the dogs barking and at times chasing things. This would make me so scared, but even more so, are the nights when we had to go down to the water tank to fetch water in the middle of the night. I would shake like a leaf at the thought of ghosts or bad men coming out of the bushes to get us.

Not only that, but as a child, I walked home from school by myself every evening. When I reached to a certain point of the way, anxiety would come upon me, and my heart would start to beat out of my chest. Every evening as I reached that certain point of the way, I would just start to scream at the top of my lungs. Anyone within a five-mile radius could usually hear me screaming from being fearful. And even now, as I'm writing, I remember the point where I started screaming every evening; the very place where I had suffered several attempted rapes.

As a child, I had a vivid imagination and the enemy capitalized on it. I saw things that were not there, and would imagine bad things happening to me on a daily basis. I was so fearful that I wouldn't even get up at nights to use the restroom and as a result, suffered the consequences in the mornings. The enemy really had a field day with my life as a child.

Experiencing these things night-after-night and evening-after-evening, created an access point where the spirit of fear came into my *soul* and plagued my life. What the enemy was trying to drive home to me was that there was no protection for me, and no one loved me enough to protect me.

The word of God tells us that there is no fear in love, but perfect love casts out all fear, because fear has to do with punishment/torment. The one who fears has not been made perfect in love **(1Jn 4:18)**.

Fear is a lie appearing to be real. People who are fearful, usually deal with anger, hopelessness, doubt and unbelief. Fear also comes with torment. It tells lies to the mind expecting you to believe them. Fear will take away your hope, and keep you stuck. The word of God tells us that God has not given us the spirit of fear, but of the spirit of love, the spirit of power and the spirit of a sound mind **(2 Tm.1:7)**.

The first step in getting rid of fear is to know that God loves you. As human beings when we love someone, we will do anything to protect them. God's love is far beyond any human love. His love is beyond our ability to measure; it has no boundaries. In the case of God loving us, He proved His love for us by giving His only beloved son as an atoning sacrifice for our sins.

There is a state of being in perfect love when we are Children of God. In this state, we come to know that God loves us, and because He loves us so much, He will protect us at all costs. The word says, *"Whoever does not love does not know God, because God is love."* — **1 Jn. 4:8**. The word of God also tells us that as Children of God we were given this love by way of the Holy Spirit, therefore, we ought to walk in love towards one another. When we find ourselves in this state of perfect love, it fights against all our fears and wins.

If you have been struggling with fear (the spirit of fear), spend some time in the book of 1 John. Here are some scriptures that we use against fear

"For God hath not given us the spirit of fear; but of power, and of love, and of a sound mind." — **2 Tm. 1:7(KJV)**.

"As the mountains surround Jerusalem, so the Lord surrounds his people both now and forevermore." — **Ps. 125:2**.

These scriptures are the word of God, and they are weapons that we use against fear.

"The Lord is my light and my salvation-whom shall I fear? The Lord is the stronghold of my life-of whom shall I be afraid?" — **Ps. 27:1**.

If we should look at the word stronghold, it represents a place that has been fortified to protect against attacks. A stronghold in this context is a secure place or a refuge, it is a place of defense.

We must get our deliverance from fear or it will plague us for the rest of our lives. We are in the stronghold of God, and nothing and no one can harm us when we are in God's place of protection.

Second, take bold steps and face your fears, even in the face of being fearful. You will be surprised to see that the things that you fear most times are only shadows, lies, false evidences appearing to be real.

The story of Gideon in the Bible always stands out to me because he was hiding in fear of something that he was born to overcome and conquer. — *Read* **Jd. 6**.

In like manner, you are called by God to be more than a conqueror, an overcomer, and that is who you are; declare that over yourself until you feel your freedom from fear!

LET'S PRAY:

Father, in the Name of Jesus, I thank you that you have kept me alive for such a time as this; I thank You for protecting me. Even in times when the enemy wanted to destroy me You said, NO to the enemy. Your word tells me that You have not given me a spirit of fear, but of love, of power and of a sound mind. I am asking You to break and completely annihilate the spirit of fear from my life.

I declare Your word over my life that I have soundness of mind, and that Your love overwhelms me. I renounce fear, and I say, NO longer will fear torment me or hold me back in life. I decree that I move forward fearlessly in life, and that I run into the beautiful future that You have for me. I thank you Father for complete deliverance from fear. I claim and confess my Freedom, in Jesus Name. Amen!

Chapter 11
Breaking Generational / Emotional Curses

One morning as I was in prayer, the *Holy Spirit* began speaking to me about erasing generational memories of past traumatic experiences from the different areas of my *soul*.

The *Holy Spirit* began to show me the similarities between those who have been traumatized by certain bad experiences and those with Alzheimers. He also showed me how traumas can be passed down through generations.

First, the Holy Spirit pointed out my grandfather to me; showing me that he had issues with Alzheimers in the latter years of his life. Strangely enough, I can remember my grandfather being very forgetful, but to my sister and I, it was a way of escape for us; we welcomed it. I say that only because our grandfather was the disciplinarian in the home, which means, the bad things that we did were forgotten after a short time, and we got off the hook *scot free*.

Often, when our grandfather would forget who we or certain people who had been in our lives for a long time were, my sister and I would look at each other, wondering what was really going on with him. We actually thought that it was strange, but had no knowledge about memory loss.

Now, my Grandfather and other family members told us stories of some of the traumatic things he went through at times; strange, to say the least. We heard stories of how sharks ate his dad on a fishing trip; another story of how one woman who wanted to be married to him, poisoned four of his children; three died—as far as I know, one made it out alive. That was just two examples of some of the traumas he suffered, there are more, but suffice it to say, he suffered tremendously in life.

My mother, God rest her *soul*, suffered quite a bit of traumatic experiences as well. She shared her stories of sexual, mental, physical and emotional abuse; she encountered a lot of rejection along with other emotional issues.

One of the stories she shared with us was that of a time when her grandmother's husband took her fishing with him. She described the torment and sheer dread she encountered, as she was left to sit in a tree for about four hours, as the alligators underneath the trees were jumping to see who could get to her first; I could understand dogs, but alligators? One can only imagine how traumatic that must have been for her and the damages it caused in her *soul*.

My mother, much like her dad, found herself experiencing memory loss before she went home to be with the Lord. This was hard for her and painful for us her children.

Again, not understanding what was really going on, we accepted what was happening to her - after all, it was a sickness that affects certain people, especially when they reached a certain age, right? No, wrong! My mother was only fifty-nine years old.

That morning, as the Spirit of God spoke to me, He began to point out what the issues really were.

Having worked in Memory Care facilities for a period of time, I came to understand that this issue the Spirit of God was talking to me about, was actually something I had witnessed, while working on that job. God allowed me to hear the stories of those with Dementia/Alzheimers, and to my surprise, they all had traumatic occurrences in their lives, at least all the ones I've encountered.

I'm in no way trying to make a medical claim or trying to diagnose any medical issues, I'm just sharing from a spiritual perspective, as I believe the Spirit of God has shown it to me.

As the Spirit of God pointed out each issue that I could remember in my life, even the things that came down through the generations, I commanded by the Spirit of God that the negative effects of each traumatic memory be erased from my *soul*, and that those areas would be healed.

The next step was to use the word of God to replace the bad memories, so that healing could come.

The *Holy Spirit* instructed me to bind up, reverse and cancel Dementia and Alzheimers and to command it to be stopped and be eradicated from my bloodline in Jesus Name.

What Studies Have Shown:

Studies have shown that doing things such as exercising, eating properly, getting enough sleep, drinking plenty of water, and reducing stressors, can help to prevent the onset of Alzheimers. However, when it comes to the past emotional traumas and the memories of them, we should turn to the workings of the Spirit of God and His Power to Deliver, Heal and Restore Our *Souls*. The Spirit of God can do what natural practices cannot.

Being in a domestically violent relationship, I was beaten constantly from head to toe. Years later I found that I had pains and issues all over my body and could not figure out what was going on with me. Later, as the Lord began to reveal the problems to me, I came to understand that even the tissue of the body has memory of every blow that was given to it. The pain that I began to feel in the different areas of my body, were the tissues saying; *"I remember the pain and I need healing to function normally."*

Allow me to encourage you; make the time to intentionally lay hands on yourself and command the negative effects of every traumatic memory to be divinely erased. It will be your responsibility to renew your mind, to think on things that are true, honorable, right, pure, lovely, and admirable according to **Phil. 4**. The word of God is able to do what psychologists, doctors and medication cannot do. So, spend time in His word; it is able to Save your *soul*.

PRAYER:

Father, in the Name of Jesus Christ, I surrender my NOW to You. Whatever went on in the generations before me, I surrender to You also. I renounce every negative generational emotion that would cause further affliction to me or the generations ahead. I come in agreement with heaven and I say, every generational spirit of brokenness, affliction, premature death is broken by the Power of the Name of Jesus Christ. I thank You for complete liberty from Alzheimers and Dementia. I thank You that every memory of physical and emotional abuse is erased from my tissue and my internal hard drive. I give You thanks that I will live a long life and will remember and tell of Your goodness to the next generation. In Jesus Name I pray. Amen!

Chapter 12
The Sanctified Soul

Esther was a woman who was considered as set apart for a special purpose. God had chosen her at that time to bring deliverance to the Jewish people. Esther, along with other young women, had to go through the process of being set apart, sanctified, and prepared to encounter the King. They had to go through a twelve months process, which was a part of the regulations for the women in those days. Their preparation process for beautifying the women, consisted of six months with oil of myrrh and six months with perfumes and cosmetics. — *Read* **Est. 2:12**. When the women went in to see the King, he only requested the one he delighted in.

In like manner, God has requested us by name. And unlike an earthly king, God, the King of kings, has chosen us and has set us apart for His special purpose. We don't have to get prepared to be chosen by God, instead, we prepare ourselves for Him, because He has already chosen us and has set us apart for His special purpose.

Much like Esther, we have been chosen by God for such a time as this. As a result, there are some disciplines that we must carry out. Because we are chosen, we cannot conduct our lives as common men often do.

For us to have a sanctified *soul*, it will take discipline on our part. It means that we live devoted and consecrated lives unto God.

When a *soul* is set apart unto God, it means that we don't do what everyone else does. It means that we give God the permission to pull us aside so that He can work on us; much like Esther. Here are a few things that happen, as we are set apart for God's special purpose:

1. Our character is worked on.

    Our character is the quality that we personify as Kingdom citizens. This includes:

a. Our moral standards — how we conduct ourselves when no one is watching. We live a life of purity, and holiness, not using our freedom to live sinfully.

b. We develop fruit according to **Gl. 5:22** which is love, joy, peace, longsuffering, kindness, and faithfulness. A part of having an excellent *soul* or one that is set apart, is having fruits that are gradually being developed. Also, our temperament, behavior, and personality reflect Christ as our fruit matures. I once heard someone say, *"gifts are given, but fruits are grown."* And, *"your gifts will take you where your character will not keep you."* As a result, we see people who are gifted, but are flawed in their character, making a mess of their life and the lives of others.

2. A part of having a sanctified *soul* is to devote one's self to prayer. As we pray, our *souls* are strengthened. When we pray the word of God, I also believe that what we

pray goes through our ear gate and affects our *souls* positively.

Praying in the spirit also helps to remove the junk from our *souls* so that we can have soundness of mind. I encourage you to take time to pray in the spirit for long periods of time…if you can, it will help to deal with even the hidden areas in your *soul*.

3. A part of having a sanctified *soul* is spending quality time reading, meditating on, and studying the word of God.

   There is no way that one can spend quality time in the word and it not affect their *souls*. The Bible says, "The law of the Lord is perfect, converting the *soul*: the testimony of the Lord is sure, making wise the simple." — **Ps. 19:7*(KJV)*.** The word of God sanctifies us. — **Jn 17:17**.

4. To have a sanctified *soul* means that we stay away from anything that will corrupt the *soul*, while allowing in the things that will bring health and healing. We do not want to hold on to anything from the enemy.

PRAYER:

Father God, I thank You for who You are in my life. I thank You for setting me apart for Your purpose. I thank You that You have made me to be someone extraordinary in this life. Father, I give You permission to do whatever is necessary to help me develop a good character, and fruit that will make me into a better vessel for You. Please help me to uphold a moral standard and to live a pure life before You. Help me to spend quality time in Your word, develop a prayer life, and to stay away from anything that would corrupt my soul. I give You thanks for this, in Jesus Name I Pray. Amen!

Chapter 13
The Restored Soul

God is the one that restores, and He loves to do so. Every one of us at one time or the other have experienced a loss of some kind or have had something that was taken from us. Well, I'm excited to say that we are in a time when God has promised to restore what was taken from us by the enemy, or that which was lost.

In **Psalms 23**, it tells us that Jesus Himself will restore our *souls* and lead us in the path of righteousness; He will also prepare a table for us in the presence of our enemies. However, no matter how willing God is to restore, some of us refuse to follow until we hit rock bottom. If you have hit rock bottom and are ready to be restored, God is ready, willing and able to do just that. Simply, open your heart and your mouth and ask Jesus to restore you right now!

Let's look at some of the ways God promise in His word to restore:

1. God restores us when we repent.

    a. The Lord restores favor and blessings to the righteous according to **Psa. 5:12**.

    b. God will restore those who have been devastated or feel like they are ruined.

    c. For those of you who have been called everything except what God says about you, God is now restoring you. You shall now be called trees of righteousness and the righteousness of God in Christ.

    d. God is about to restore your favor, and your honor, in fact, He is going to restore double honor, and your inheritance. *Read* **Is. 61: 3-8**.

One of the fruit of repentance is restoration. After David had repented from his sins, he cried out to the Lord to restore back to him the joy of his salvation. However, he had to pay the consequences for his sins, and God, because of His unfailing love to His people, restored him.

God promised to restore the years and everything else that we have lost. — **Jl. 2:25,26** and He did. When Jesus came and died for our sins, everything that was lost, got restored. Therefore, when we received Jesus, we received the restoration packaged in Him.

PRAYER:

Father God, I thank You that You are always ready to restore. I ask You to restore my soul; every area of brokenness, please restore. Restore all the good things that I have lost, and what cannot be restored, please return to me. You have promised in Your word that You will restore the years that I have lost to bad relationships, years that I have lost because I made wrong decisions, years lost because of sickness, reputation that I have lost as a result of the gossip of others, and confidence that I have lost because of being undermined by others. Father, You are able to make everything work in my favor and restore me to a condition, better than I ever was. Thank You for not only restoration, but also for restitution and retribution. I set myself in agreement with Your word, and I receive Your blessing, in Jesus Name. Amen!

Chapter 14
The Merry / Joyful Soul

Christmas was some of the best times for us growing up. I could remember as a child in the Caribbean, when it came around to Christmas there was always an unusual sense of joy and expectation in the air.

Right around Christmas, people's attitudes would be better, they were more giving and festive, hope came alive, and there was peace all around. It was usually a time when we dressed in our best just because of the special season. In other words, it was a happy and joyful time.

We realize that people go through struggles and at times, damaging, and painful situations that make them sad. This is what the word of God says, *"A cheerful heart is good medicine, but a crushed spirit dries up the bones."* — **Pr.17:22**.

Facts about Broken Heart Syndrome: *"Profound emotional sadness doesn't just weigh heavy on your mind. It significantly impacts your body."*[10] **Deborah Serani Psy.D**.

Having a merry heart/*soul* or being happy is a state of mind and we tend to fluctuate based one what's going on in the moment. However, there is a perpetual joy that resides in our spirits that we can always pull on to give us strength, even in times that are not so merry. This kind of Joy comes from God and it is designed to give us hope and keep us strong in spite of what's going on.

God wants us to have confident expectation in Him that no matter what, we can pull on the spirit of joy that He has placed in us by way of His Spirit.

Let's look at some things that activate our joy and help us to keep a joyful heart (*soul*).

---

[10] https://www.psychologytoday.com/blog/two-takes-depression/201102/broken-heart-syndrome

1. Having Faith in God.

   We have never seen a person who is full of Faith and is sad at the same time. Sadness is basically saying that there is no hope. Not to say, that people don't get sad at times, however, with Faith in God, you cannot stay sad. The word of God says, *"Now Faith is the substance of things hoped for, the evidence of things not seen." is the evidence of things not seen"* — **Heb.11:1**. Therefore, where Faith is, hope is also present; because we believe God, we hope in Him also.

2. Answered prayers or fulfilled desires.

   "Hope deferred maketh the heart sick: but when the desire cometh, it is a tree of life"— **Pr. 13:12(KJV)**.

   When an expectation is delayed, it usually makes one disappointed. If there are continual disappointments, then it usually leads to sadness. When that expectation is met, whether by way of answered prayers or a desire fulfilled, it brings joy. For some of us, what gives us the confidence that God is hearing and is pleased with us, is when our prayers or our expectation is answered; it makes us joyful.

3. When you refresh others, you get joy from it also.

   Have you ever encouraged someone in a time when you yourself needed encouragement, and found that you became joyful and strengthened as well? Why? God created it so. God wants us to encourage one another and bear one another's burdens; there is a blessing in that. This is what the word of God says,

   "Nehemiah said, 'Go and enjoy choice food and sweet drinks, and send some to those who have nothing prepared. This day is holy to our Lord. Do not grieve, for the joy of the Lord is your strength.'" — **Neh.8:10**.

4. Spending time in God's Presence.

   If we spend time in the word, Thanking God, or Praising Him, we cannot remain sad. Doing all these things, often brings us in the Presence of the Lord, and there is no sadness in His Presence. **Ps. 16:11** says — that in His Presence there is fullness of Joy and at His right hand there are pleasures forevermore. So, if you are looking for joy, spend time in the Presence of God.

5. Finding purpose to one's life brings joy.

There is no one sadder than those who believe that there is no purpose to their lives. So many have fallen into depression and have even ended their lives believing that there was no point in going on.

Finding purpose to your life starts with finding the one who Created you. Many times, we see in the Bible where someone encountered Christ, and was given a new identity. New in the sense that we sometimes label ourselves as we see ourselves, we also label ourselves as others have labeled us- and unfortunately most of the times they are the wrong labels. The beginning of **Ps. 16:11***(KJV)* — says, *"Thou wilt shew me the path of life:"* and for God to show us anything, we must first spend quality time with Him. Once we have found purpose, we then become joyful, and impactful in helping others.

PRAYER

Father, I thank You that all power is in Your hand, and that I am in Your hand too. Where I have sinned against You, please forgive me and restore my joy. Lord, where I have been disappointed, please give me hope again. Deliver me from sadness and give me a glad heart. Your word says, that a merry heart does good like medicine, so please let my bones rejoice. Father, please break me out of the captivity of sadness, and cause me to dream again. Father, please fill my mouth with laughter and my tongue with singing. Cause me to be a blessing to others in their times of need, and I thank You that I will reap in joy. I declare joy and gladness over my life and the lives of those whom I come in contact with. I thank You for the oil of joy, instead of the spirit of heaviness. I thank You for Your joy which gives me strength. All this I ask, in Jesus Name I Pray. Amen!

Chapter 15
The Freed Soul

Who told you that you are not Free? Are you in Christ? If so, then you are Free. You may not be walking in your Freedom, or you may have forfeited it through doors you have opened to the enemy, but according to the word of God, those whom the son of God has set Free are indeed Free. — **Jn. 8:36**.

Since Christ has made you Free, then the enemy has no legal right to hold you or I in any form of bondage; rather, we must fight to walk in freedom. *Martin Luther King, Jr* said, *"Freedom is never voluntarily given by the oppressor; it must be demanded by the oppressed."* Why should it be demanded? Because, Christ has made us Free.

Walking in total freedom doesn't mean we are exempt from struggles and situations. However, what it does mean, is in spite of our situations or struggles, we know that we are not bound.

This is what the word of God says,

"It is for freedom that Christ has set us free. Stand firm, then, and do not let yourselves be burdened again by a yoke of slavery." — **Gl. 5:1**.

Basically, what Paul is saying is that we have a choice in the matter. If we are not comfortable in something, the first thing that we will do is to seek our freedom; likewise, with our *souls*, if there is something that is preventing us from walking in freedom we must seek to be Free.

How do we seek to be Free or to keep our freedom? Declare what God has already said about your freedom, for example, because Christ has already paid the full price for my freedom, I decree that I am Free according to **Is. 53:5** and **Gl. 5:1**. Sometimes, our freedom is locked up in our mouths. The word of God tells us in **Jb. 22:28** — that we shall make a decree about a thing and it shall be established unto us, and not just that, but light also shall shine upon our ways. In other words, you will begin to have revelation of your freedom.

Another way that we begin to walk in our freedom is to get rid of guilt and condemnation.

The spirit of condemnation is one of the things that hold many people captive illegally. The word says, if we are in Christ, condemnation does not apply to us. — **Rm.8:1**.

We walk in freedom when we turn from sin unto righteousness.

If you are in covenant with Christ and you have sinned, the first thing you do is to repent... It means to turn away from and change your mind about sinning and asking God for forgiveness. God does not hold our sins against us when we repent. In fact, He sent His son to die for us while we were yet sinners, but that is not an excuse to continue in sin.

To walk in freedom, we must learn how to constantly cast down vain imaginations.

The mind is the part of our *soul* where the enemy wars with us the most. If we don't learn how to cast down the enemy's arguments, he will use them to put and keep us in bondage. Learn how to recognize the subtle suggestions of the enemy and cast them down quickly.

Declarations:

I decree that I am Free!

I am Free from sicknesses and diseases, because Christ has redeemed me from the curse of the law; therefore, my body is a disease-free zone. — **Gl. 3:13**.

I am Free from condemnation and guilt, because I walk in the spirit, therefore, I will not fulfill the lust of the flesh. — **Gl. 5:16**.

I am Free from negative thoughts, because I think only on things that are true, honorable, right, pure, lovely and admirable. — **Php. 4:8**.

I am Free from poverty, because I prosper and walk in health as my *soul* is prospering. — **3Jn 2**.

I am Free from fear, because God has not given me the spirit of fear, but of love, of power and of a sound mind. — **2Tm. 1:7**.

I am Free from sin, because I have been redeemed through the blood of Jesus. — **Col 1:14**.

I am Free from guilt and shame, because God has caused me to forget the shame of my youth. — **Is. 54:4**.

I am Free from anxiety, because I have cast all my cares upon the Lord and He cares for me. — **1Pt. 5:7**.

I am Free from every trap of the enemy, because God has given His angels charge over me to keep me. — **Ps. 91:11**.

I am Free from every form of bondage, because the son of God has made me Free. — **Jn 8:36**.

PRAYER:

Father, in Jesus Name I come to You. You promised in Your word that whom the son has set free, is free indeed; therefore, I claim Your word over my life and the lives of my loved ones. Father please deliver us from everything that will cause bondage in our lives. Free me from the memories of past negative experiences that have held me in bondage. Free me from fear, shame, and condemnation. Free me from all infirmities. Free me from poverty and a poverty mindset. Help me to use Your word to combat every situation that would try to keep me in bondage. This I Pray, in Jesus Name. Amen!

Chapter 16
The Healed Soul

Whether we have experienced physical ailments in the past or we are experiencing them now, we must realize that most times they are rooted in toxic emotions or some form of traumatic experience. Bad emotions such as unforgiveness, resentment, offense, envy, bitterness, disappointment, fear, anger etc. opens the door for the enemy to come in and destroy our health.

Remember, the word of God tells us that as it is with our *souls*, so it is with our health. Perhaps, the issues that we have had with our health are really *soul* issues.

Studies have shown that certain ailments such as cancer, diabetes, asthma, allergies, migraine headaches, ulcers, and pain in the different parts of the body, can be traced back to some emotional wound that we have not dealt with.

The word of God tells us that by the stripes of Jesus Christ we were healed. So then, why do we see people asking for prayer concerning their health, and not receiving healing? Is it because the word of God doesn't work? There is no doubt that the problem is not God's word. God is faithful to all of His Promises. His word is already settled in heaven, and nothing can change that. We however are the ones who have to adjust to what the word of God says.

One of the major reasons we don't receive or maintain our healing, is because we have to forgive. We must let go of bitterness, anger, resentment and offense. Then, we will begin to see the manifestation of healing in our bodies.

God has made provision for our healing. He is *Jehovah Rapha- "The Lord who heals."* When the children of Israel were delivered from bondage in Egypt, God made a covenant with them. **Ex. 15:26** — *"If you listen carefully to the Lord your God and do what is right in his eyes, if* *you pay attention to his commands and keep all his decrees, I will not bring on you any of the diseases I brought on the Egyptians, for I am the Lord, who heals you."*

We all have definitely fallen short in keeping God's commands and statues; therefore, we should reap a harvest of sickness and diseases; but Christ came and took the punishment for us. The word of God says, *"But he was wounded for our transgressions, He was bruised for our iniquities: the chastisement of our peace was upon him; and with his stripes we are healed."* **Is. 53:5(KJV)**.

Let us confess our sins, let go of hurt and what people have done to us so that we can receive our healing. Confess the word of God daily concerning your healing and trust God to do His part according to His word. Let's pray:

PRAYER:

Father, in Jesus Name, I thank You for being my Jehovah Rapha. Today I let go of all bitterness, unforgiveness, resentment and pride and I ask You to forgive me for my sin of rebellion against You and Your word. Thank You for making provision for my healing by way of Jesus Christ. Thank You, Lord, that You were wounded for my transgressions, You were bruised for my iniquities, the chastisement of my peace was upon You, and by Your stripes I confess that I am healed and made whole, body and soul. Thank You Father, for being gracious to me and for being my strength. Thank You for Your peace in my mind, body and spirit concerning my healing in Jesus Name. Amen!

Chapter 17
Commanding Wholeness in your Soul

Father, in the name of Jesus Christ, and by the authority of Your word, I command healing and wholeness in my *soul*!

I speak to every issue that is creating havoc in my *soulish* realm and I command it to be uprooted in the Name of Jesus!

I speak to every hidden place in my *soul* and I say, the light of Jesus Christ exposes hidden spirits of wounds, rejection, pride, infirmities, bitterness and offense, in Jesus Name!

Every spirit hidden in my *soul*, I command you to come out now. In Jesus Name!

Every spirit of oppression that is oppressing my *soul*, come out now in Jesus Name!

I declare I have freedom from past hurts, pain, and traumas in Jesus Name!

I declare that my *soul* is being restored according to **Ps. 23:3**. I say I have maximum restoration in Jesus Name!

My *soul* blesses you O' my God, and I will not forget Your benefits; You forgive all my sins and You heal all my diseases.

You have redeemed my life from destruction and crowned me with Your loving kindness and tender mercies. **Ps. 103:1**.

I decree that every destructive pattern, attitude, behavior, and mindset is broken in Jesus Name!

Father, I speak your word of health and healing to my body and in every area of my *soul*, and I claim Your promises for abundance of peace and security for my mind, in Jesus Name! —**Jr. 33:6**

I decree that I prosper and experience good health, because my *soul* is prospering, in Jesus Name!

I command every unhealthy *soul* tie in my life to be broken, and every ungodly relationship that keeps my *soul* in bondage to be severed by the blood of Jesus Christ.

I declare that my *soul* escapes as a bird out of the snares of the fowlers; the snare is broken and I have escaped in Jesus Mighty Name! — **Ps. 124:7**

I break the power of every word that was released against my *soul* to destroy, hinder or to stop me. I say those words are broken, rendered null and void; they will not accomplish what they were sent to do in Jesus Mighty Name!

"Many are saying of me, 'God will not deliver him.' But you, Lord, are a shield around me, my glory, the One who lifts my head high." In Jesus Name! — **Ps. 3:2,3**.

I speak to my *soul*, and I say do not be cast down, put your hope in God. In Jesus Name!

I declare that as I look into your perfect law, my *soul* is converted and refreshed in Jesus Name! — **Ps. 19:7**.

I declare that as I walk in Your path, I find rest for my *soul*, in Jesus Name! — **Jr. 6:16**.

Father, release an anointing to destroy yokes and lift burdens. I take on your yoke and I learn of you, and I find rest for my *soul*. **Mt. 11:29**

My *soul* magnifies you O' my Lord. —**Lk. 1:46**.

Thank You Lord that Your word helps my *soul* and brings healing to my bones, in Jesus Name!

I am fearfully and wonderfully made, and that my *soul* knows very well.

Thank You Father that you are the lover of my *soul* in Jesus Name!

I decree that I have a new lease on life.

I am blessed and highly favored by God.

God's favor surrounds me as a shield.

I lack no good thing, because God is restoring all good things to me, in Jesus Name!

I declare that I shall overtake and recover all in Jesus Name!

I declare that I prosper and I am in good health, because now my *soul* is prospering in Jesus Name. Amen!

Fresh Wind:

For you who have gone through much pain and shame as a result of being wounded, God is going to give you double for your trouble, and double honor for your shame. He is about to restore to you what the enemy has stolen; your innocence, your peace, your confidence, your joy, your money, your health and more.

No longer will you discount yourself based on what you have been through or how others have judged you; instead, look to God with expectancy for your healing.

I declare that the *fresh wind* of God's Spirit (the Ruach of God) is coming upon you to blow out everything and everyone that does not belong in your lives in this season. He is healing you, refreshing you and strengthening you to reign in the seasons to come. Get up! Shake the ashes off, this is a new day for you! Salvation has come unto to you today, receive it in Jesus Name. Amen!

Chapter 18
No More Condemnation

There are so many promises that were given to us as Believers, and so often we have not seen the manifestation of them in our lives. There are times when we fast, pray, and give according to scriptures, but have still experienced limitations.

As the Lord began to connect the dots to this puzzle, He showed me where some of us are faulty in our thinking as a result of lies that were planted by the enemy. First, many of us struggle with condemnation in our *souls*. When there is condemnation, it leaves us having no confidence at all in God. Condemnation tells us that God doesn't love us, it says things like, *"God loves Mary and Suzie and will do more for them than for me"* or in other cases we believe the worst about us and see others as more valuable than we are.

If we are honest, there are times when we pray for others and they see results; we believe God for others and see their breakthroughs but fall short when it comes to us getting our requests. The reason for this is condemnation. This is what the word says, *"Dear friends, if our hearts do not condemn us, we have confidence before God and receive from him anything we ask, because we keep His commands and do what pleases Him."* — **1 Jn. 3:21,22**.

The solution to breakthrough in this area is to get rid of condemnation. If you have been born of God, condemnation is not your portion, *"Therefore, there is now no condemnation for those who are in Christ Jesus,"* — **Rm. 8:1**.

Now is the time that we begin to uproot every faulty belief system deeply embedded in our *souls*... and as we do so, we must begin to plant the Truth of God's word and watch them grow into awesome breakthroughs and answered prayers.

Daily Confessions:

God Loves Me

God Cares for Me

I am God's Friend

I am God's Beloved

God is not upset with Me

He Approves of Me

All His Promises are Yes to Me

God Favors Me

His Provisions are Mine

Healing is Mine

PRAYER:

Father, I thank You that I am born of You, and because I am of You, there is no condemnation to me. I speak to every area of condemnation in my soul and I command You to be uprooted in Jesus Name. I am loved, accepted and approved by You Father and for that reason I thank You. Every promise that I forfeited as a result of condemnation, I ask You to restore to me. I thank you Father every promise that You have given me will come to pass in my life. Thank You Father that every need is met in my life and my future is beautiful and bright in Jesus Name I Pray, Amen!

Chapter 19
Being Transparent: My Story

As children of God, we must be aware that we are not in a competition. God's Will is that we are so built up in Him that we are able to build His kingdom and impact the world for Jesus Christ. Our individual processes and testimonies are what qualifies us to impact others. We must never negate the process which brought us to where we are in life. God gives us grace, and He allows in our lives only what He will use to be a blessing to others and ultimately bring Him Glory.

This is my testimony:

I grew up on the Island of Jamaica with grandparents who loved the Lord and were great examples to us. My mother left my sister and I when we were two years and two months old. Although we had good grandparents, I still encountered bad people with terrible issues.

From an early age, I knew what it was to be physically, verbally, and sexually abused. At the age of seven, I was brutally raped, beaten, and left alone in a pig pen. After that incident, sexual and physical abuse became a constant thing for me to experience; it had become the norm for me as I was growing up. Whenever I wasn't trying to overcome the aftermath of a rape, I was trying to get away from a rapist.

At the age of sixteen I came to the United States where the trend of abuse continued in my life. My first job at one of the largest food chains in America and around the world, was where I was gang raped and left with extreme shame and more brokenness than I could deal with. After a while, I went into a depression so deep that I quit school, chained smoked, and slept. A great portion of my late teenage years to early adulthood was spent in bed, because I was too broken to face the world.

After a while, I started going to parties where I met the man who eventually became my children's father and later on my husband.

Eventually, he became ***Abusive***.

For about nineteen years, I stayed with someone who almost took my life. I didn't know how to get out, because of fear for my life and the fear of having my children taken from me. Many times, the abuse took me to near death experiences, but God kept me. After all those years, God took me from the relationship and helped me and my children hide in another state.

My husband met a woman who had six children; and full-blown AIDS, but didn't tell him, and consequently, he contracted the virus. I had no clue what was going on at the time, and secretly wanted to call him to come back into our lives.

God gave me a dream that scared me away from making that decision and also gave me a sense of urgency in my spirit to divorce him which I did. I filed for divorce and in less than a month the courts granted my request. About three weeks after divorcing him, I found out he allegedly shot the lady in her head and killed her, and then he committed suicide.

Life for me went on, but it wasn't without great anguish, woundedness, guilt, depression and all the negative emotions that one can imagine.

My *soul* was so damaged, I had no hope, and no passion. I couldn't see a moment past the minute that I was in. Rejection was one of the feelings I suffered with greatly. God has been faithful to me. He has kept me, delivered, and is delivering me from the effects of those traumatic events. He has also allowed me to encourage countless others to let them know that there is hope after hopeless situations.

Nothing that you and I have gone through in this life has to take our hope. God knows how to make all things work together for our good and the betterment of others.

You may have gone through some tough experiences in your life and feel like all hope is gone. You may feel as if God is not with you or you may be wondering why He allowed certain things to happen to you. Know that God is a Good Father, but also consider the fact that we live in a fallen world with people who are controlled by a devil.

Be encouraged, God is with you and He has always been with you. The reason you and I are still here, is because God is with us, He has been protecting us, and has Great Plans and Purposes for our lives.

I pray that this book has ministered to you in more ways than one.

Thanks again for reading. May the Grace and Peace of God be multiplied in your life and the lives of your loved ones. May the road ahead of you be cleared of all obstacles. May you experience the love of God in such a beautiful way that it transforms you. May you break Free from everything that held you back in the past, and may you fulfill the Purpose for which you were born in Jesus Name!

ALSO, BY DENVA SMITH:

Still Standing but by God's Grace

*Moving Forward:
Walking Out of Bondage Into Freedom*

www.ingramcontent.com/pod-product-compliance
Lightning Source LLC
Chambersburg PA
CBHW071126090426
42736CB00012B/2024